SCREEN-FREE SUMMER

Endless Ideas to Get Kids off the
Device and into the Season

Copyright © 2017 by Keri Middaugh

DISCLAIMER

The information in the following pages is intended only for informational purposes and no guarantee is made as to its efficacy. It is presented without assurance regarding its prolonged validity or interim quality. There are no scenarios in which the publisher or the original author of this work can be in any fashion deemed liable for any hardship or damages that may befall them after undertaking information described herein. Read and implement at your own risk. It will probably be awesome.

ACKNOWLEDGEMENTS

Many thanks to all the families that have trusted us enough to go along with these ideas over the years, including the Billman, Brokaw, Dority, Edwards, Ekpiken, Evans, Fox, Gehrke, Gimotty, Goehmann, Harris, Heffley, Hill, Ibarguen, Lange, Lorenz, Malmer, Miklosovic, Morris, Ramade, Ross, Scanio, Van Zomeren, and Zapor families. It's been fun, hasn't it?

TABLE OF CONTENTS

Then followed that beautiful season... Summer...

Filled was the air with a dreamy and magical light; and the land-
scape

Lay as if new created in all the freshness of childhood.

—HENRY WADSWORTH LONGFELLOW

INTRODUCTION, CAVEATS, AND GENERAL ENCOURAGEMENTS

What follows is neither a philosophy nor a manifesto. It is simply a manual chock full of ideas of how to use the wide expanse of June, July, and August, what we fondly call "summer" in the Northern Hemisphere. At our home we always aim to spend more time off the devices during summer months, but as soon as the last school bell rings, we find ourselves at a loss for ideas. So this year, we decided to do something about it, and **this book is the result.**

Screen-free is not a punishment, but an opportunity. Studies have shown that kids with less screen time read more, are more active, and engage with the world around them in a deeper way. One family reported that their children bickered less and were more good-natured when they gave up devices for several weeks. Experts even say that a little bit of boredom gives children the space to develop creativity and initiative. As long as idle hands are not throwing rocks at windows or tormenting the neighbor's cat, we let our kids experience a bit of boredom now and them.

We think it's important to watch out for the "vice" in "device." It has been shown that screens can be addictive, both for kids and adults. We also know that addicts get grumpy when they don't get their fix. We encourage families to offer something better than devices, such as an outing, a skill, or the wonderland of their own imaginations. This may take some getting used to, but we believe that time away from the computer is worth it in the end.

We would be remiss not to acknowledge the irony that many readers will read this very book on a device. Fine. No problem. **What comes afterward is the important part.**

Please treat this book like you would a buffet: **take what pleases you and leave the rest behind**. What seems fun to one family may leave another family yawning. No big deal. Feel free to modify to accommodate kids from toddlers to teenagers. Our family consists of two parents and two middle school aged daughters, a family dog, and a small flock of backyard hens. And we try to live frugally. We live in a small city that has a river, a university, a handful of museums and restaurants. Within 30 miles we have 2 large cities which are rich cultural centers, as well as a few lakes. That's where we're coming from. **So use this book as a springboard.** We invite you to come up with your own screen-free ideas and post them on _our facebook page, Screen-Free Summer: Endless Ideas book._ Yes, you'll have to sneak some screen time for this. Feel free to post photos of your families engaging in some of these activities. Or better yet, don't post on the facebook page. Instead, tell your friend or neighbor about it and encourage them!

Let us also say that the Internet is wonderful. Tablets are convenient. And smartphones are becoming indispensable. They are our cameras, our calendars, our cookbooks. They are our newspapers, our maps, our pony express. They entertain, organize, teach. But they are not everything. **We feel that much of the memories of life, most of the lessons, are experienced away from screens.** One idea is to use online resources to plan the week (consulting maps, museum hours, recipes, etc.) during a designated research time. We can model using screens as a way to have access to information. Then step away from the screen. **Let's help our families get off the device and into the season!**

> **Extra Challenge,** an idea that aims to stretch you even further!

1

LIFE SKILLS

Our children all have one thing in common: they are on the road to becoming adults. And it's our job to prepare them for that eventuality. Thankfully we have teachers, grandparents, and others in the community who also sow into our children. The point of this book is to support families in giving kids meaningful face-to-face, hand-to-hand experiences that will be a formational part of their childhood, without relying on the ubiquitous device.

I have one friend who claims her main role as a parent is to prepare her children to be decent roommates. Courteous, tidy, generally not too annoying. She's got a point. For a while we had a rule at our house: anyone who complains of boredom gets a chore to do. If kids can learn to operate a device that relies on invisible ether, they can learn to operate a washing machine. Yes, they might need a stepstool and a little coaching, but we're fine with that.

- **Laundry**. We once heard a radio show that said a great way to get high school sophomores ready for college is to have them do their own laundry because it requires planning and seeing a multi-step process through to completion. We say, "Why wait till sophomore year?" Get the child a hamper in his/her favorite color and learn that skill today.

- **Dishes.** By machine or by hand, this task is relentless because about every 4 hours or so, it seems a meal is necessary.

- **Order for themselves at a restaurant.** Depending on the shyness of your child, this might take some level of coaxing. Remind them that a smile, along with a "please" and "thank you" goes a long way.

- **Take out trash and recycling bins.** Little ones can empty waste-baskets. This can also be an opportunity to discuss ways to reduce waste in our daily lives.

- **Set the table for a meal and clear it afterward.** Little children can do this. Paper placemats that have the shapes of the items in their proper places are just fine. Kids can even make them beforehand by tracing around the utensils and plate.

- **Prepare the meal.** Older kids can do this. See chapter on *New Foods* for more ideas.

- **Cut the grass.** Best for older kids, and could even turn into a business. With a good mix of sunny and rainy weather, this skill is needed every week or so.

- **Pull weeds.** There is always another weed to pull, so get those kids involved. Focused weeding can yield big results in a small amount of time, so coax reluctant weeders into the garden for the length of two or three songs on the radio.

- **Clean bathrooms.** There is a bit of family folklore that says when toddlers try to play in the toilet, it's time to hand them a scrub brush and show them how to use it. There is something strangely satisfying about a clean mirror, sink, and toilet. Even a child can enjoy this.

- **Vacuum.** A tidy floor is better for building cushion forts!

- **Dust.** A clean surface is better for displaying shells, acorns, and other treasures.

- **Scrub the floors.** One child can squirt the floor with a 50/50 solution of vinegar and water, while another child follows behind, "skating" with a microfiber cloth under each foot. Or turn on the music for a clean-the-floor-dance-party.

- **Pump gas.** News flash: kids don't have to be 16 to do this! And it will sure come in handy when they do get their license later on. Be sure they notice how much the tank of gas costs, and how much that translates to in terms of number of dogs walked, number of lawns mowed, or whatever they are currently doing to earn money.

- **Wash the car.** Don't forget to vacuum the inside and wipe the dashboard.

- **Walk the dog.** "A tired dog is a good dog," so take that Fido around the block.

- **Check the smoke alarms.** Make sure the battery is working and review the family escape plan. This hit home with us recently when we lost one of our dear neighbors in a house fire. We promptly taught the children how to remove their bedroom window screens and climb out onto the roof right below. We hope to never use this skill, but we're confident that this simple training is worthwhile.

- **Balance the checkbook.** Done alongside an adult, this skill is one that kids likely won't learn in school but they will invariably need. Talk to them about budgets, living below one's means, and wise planning for future expenses.

- **Talk to strangers appropriately.** Kids need to be able to advocate for themselves and ask for help from trustworthy adults. So encourage those kids to ask librarians to help them find the materials they need (see the Map Work section in the *Unschooling* chapter). Give them some cash and send them to a nearby store with a list of 4 or 5 simple items to purchase. If kids aren't quite ready for this, teach them to do something smaller, like answer the phone or deliver the mail to a neighbor when it accidentally ended up in your mailbox.

Extra challenge: Have a leaky faucet or a toilet that runs too long? Get out the tool box and fix these together.

2

DAY TRIPS

Summer affords us more free time, more relaxed schedules, and the wide expanse of the day. Grab a map and hop in the car. Day trips can be an opportunity to combine several ideas in this book and make a whole scrapbook of memories at once. Get the kids on board by giving them say on where to go.

- **Capital city.** Ours is about 90 minutes away by car. There is something very patriotic about seeing the white dome of the capitol building, and many capitols have tours available.

- **Nearby lake/river/ocean.** Our town has a nice riverfront, but when we're looking for something new, we can drive an hour or two and be near a sizeable body of water with a proper beach. What's within an hour's drive of you?

- **Museums.** Natural History, Science, Hands On, Modern Art, Firehouse, Automotive, Arab American. These are a selection of the museums out here. Many libraries have day passes for patrons to check out, which will keep admission prices down. A postcard from the gift shop is an affordable momento.

- **Waterpark/spraypark.** For our family, summer doesn't seem like summer unless we make that trip to the waterpark. Ours is small and sweet and makes a nice outing for the day. When the kids were toddlers, we opted for the spraypark in the next town over.

- **Zoo.** Want to see a giraffe, a penguin, a gorilla? Summer is your chance to visit these amazing creatures. Snack on peanuts in their shell for a retro experience.

Extra challenge: Plan & execute a tour of fried chicken places, music shops, covered bridges, or other element that especially pleases you.

3

ROAD TRIPS

Join the many Americans who take to the road in the summer. We drive to experience mountains, sand dunes, amusement parks, the largest ball of twine. What are you waiting for? By the time kids reach age 10 (the perfect road trip age, in our opinion), they only have 8 more summers with you (before adulthood, that is). One family we know sat their 10 year old down and asked him to make a list of 8 places he would love to visit, then they tackled one each year.

- **Near or far, staying overnight is fun.** Even a local bed and breakfast can be a memorable event.

- **Plan a route with paper maps.** Kids can use a photocopy to trace distances covered with a highlighter.

- **Get a stack of books from the library about the destination.** Is there a historical component, a geological feature, something else notable?

- **Camping/glamping.** While not our personal cup of tea, people claim to love camping and you can make it as cushy as you like.

- **Start a collection.** Collect one rock/keychain/shell/postcard from every city you visit. Photos might be the best collectible for the minimalists among us.

- Not a fan of driving? **The Amtrak train** makes traveling easy, and passengers can read, sleep, and walk around during the trip. **The Megabus** is also an option, and if you book early enough, you just might score one of those $1 tickets.

Extra challenge: Try to visit all mom-and-pop places along the way. No chain restaurants allowed. Bonus for you if you strike up a conversation with the owner.

4

START A BUSINESS

With all the free time that summer affords, kids can be encouraged to start a little business. It may last one afternoon or a few years, but the lessons learned are worth the effort. Words to introduce: sales, profit, expenses, start-up costs, advertising, customer satisfaction, brick-and-mortar. Opportunities also arise for them to deposit their earnings and interact with the bank teller. Here are some age-appropriate business ideas.

- **Lemonade stand.** When a parent hands you a sack of lemons….. How about pink lemonade too?

- **Popcorn stand.** In addition to butter and salt, you could try creating other flavors (vanilla, caramel, chocolate, sriracha, curry).

- **Car wash/detailing.** Kids can wash the family car, then expand to neighbors, then regular clients in business parking lots. Make sure those towels never touch the ground. No one wants a scratched paint job, even from enterprising children.

- **Cut grass.** Again, practice on your own grass, then approach the neighbors.

- **Babysitting/mother's helper/dad's helper.** Older kids can be a big help to families with little ones.

- **Dog walking**. "A tired dog is a good dog." And families don't always have time to give Fido the exercise he needs. Bring doggie bags!

- **Tutor, homework helper, book buddy.** Older kids have more skills than they realize, especially when compared to emerging readers or kids struggling with multiplication facts. Parents may be happy to pay for an older child to encourage a younger child in his/her studies.

- **Chauffer.** A responsible teen with a driver's license can shuttle kids to their lessons, playdates, and camps.

- **Errand runner.** Many busy families will pay good money to not have to stand in line at the post office, pharmacy, or other mundane places.

- **Organizer**. Does your child have a knack for efficiency, prioritization, and organization? They could help people organize their pantries, closets, basements. They could also be put to work helping a household pack up for a move.

Extra challenge: Use earnings to fund a road trip or a camp of your choice.

5

CAMPS!

Many families plan camps first and everything else after, and we can see why. Camps are so fun! They are taught by an expert, gather like-minded kids, and develop great skills. Sending kids to camps can get pricey, so plan accordingly. In our family, kids and parents split the cost, with the kids using their dog-walking money to cover their part. As a bonus, this gives both kids and parents some time away from each other and time with others who care about them. Distance makes the heart grow fonder, right? Here are just a few campy ideas:

- Art

- Drama

- Nature skills

- Sports

- Music

- Bible School

- Meditation or yoga

- **STEM**. Science, technology, engineering, math-focused activities.

- **Zoology**. Yes, there is one in our area.

- **Mommy/Daddy Camp.** This is a fun idea for families with younger kids or a tight budget. For part of the day, the kids are with one parent who organizes activities according to his/her strengths. Then for another chunk of the day, the kids are with the other parent for other activities. In our house, that looked like kitchen fun and library time for Mommy Camp in the morning. Then music time or a trip to the park for Daddy Camp in the afternoon.

Extra challenge: Not finding a camp you're looking for? Start your own! This can be as simple as inviting an extra child over for focused activities, or as involved as getting licensed, creating a website, and starting a whole new enterprise.

6

VINTAGE FUN

As long as we are stepping away from the screen for a bit, it's not that far of a jump to step back in history. We have found that many of these old fashioned games keep us active, develop memory skills, or facilitate family time. Ask grandparents or elderly neighbors if they've played any of these.

- **Jump rope, with rhymes.** Our library has a book of jump rope rhymes, and once we tire of these, we modify them with more current lyrics.

- **Double Dutch jump rope.** If you are looking for a fun, rhythmic challenge, try double dutch. Practice makes progress on this one!

- **Jacks.** Ask a grandparent about this hand-eye coordination game.

- **Hopscotch**. Finally put to use all that sidewalk chalk that gathers in the foyer closet.

- **Drive-in movie.** Because these are a dying breed, you'll have to research to find a drive-in movie theater, but it will be worth it. Another option is to hang a sheet over the fence and project a film there. Kids could make cars from large cardboard boxes and bring their own popcorn.

- **Hoola hoop.** Turn on some 1950s music and get moving!

- **Four Square**. As a child, I never understood the nuances of this game, but we have revived a simpler version. Draw a large square on the driveway with sidewalk chalk. Divide it into four quadrants, with a child standing in each (this may need some recruiting if neighbor kids). The leader announces a certain topic ("colors!" or "Taylor Swift songs!" for example). The children bounce a large playground ball rhythmically between each other, saying an item that belongs to the topic whenever it is their turn to bounce. If a child cannot think of one in time, he/she is out, making room for another child to come in.

- **Rollerskate/rollerblade**. Often thrift stores and garage sales will have these for sale.

- **Sack races.** Sew some simple burlap sacks or ask for them from a local coffee beanery. Or use some old pillowcases that you are willing to get dirty.

- **Square dance.** Find a local square dance club and pop in to one of their dances. Square dancing is usually family friendly, so bring a group of all ages for a good time.

- **Put together a jigsaw puzzle.** Set up a card table on a rainy day and pull out one of those puzzles that are in the closet. Try to finish in one sitting, or let it linger and come together day by day.

- **Go fly a kite.** If you are feeling ambitious, make one!

Extra challenge: Research games of ancient time periods or civilizations and play them. Now, where to get that pig's bladder?

7

VOLUNTEER

Getting out of our comfort zone and helping others in need is a great antidote for a complaining attitude, at least in our house. Plus, it's a great way to teach the word **philanthropic**. In the end, we're not sure who benefits more - us or those we're helping.

- **Soup kitchen or food pantry.** Make a family shopping trip to donate groceries, or arrange to come at mealtime to serve the people face to face.

- **Library**. Those books don't just shelve themselves. Ask at the circulation desk for volunteer opportunities for older kids.

- **Place of worship.** Kids can set up chairs, hand out bulletins, help teach lessons to younger kids, and many other useful activities.

- **Humane Society.** Dogs need walking. Cats need snuggling. There's probably also a bit of bedding that needs freshening.

- **Clean up local park**. Pick up some trash or put down some mulch.

- **Visit people in hospital.** Call first to see about visiting the children's wing. You could even bring a silly parade, coloring pages, or a mobile photo booth with funny hats.

- **Lend a hand at a working farm.** You might come home with a dozen eggs and needing a shower, but it will be a day to remember!

- **Read to a resident of a senior home or to an elderly neighbor.** Offer to dust the picture frames or play a simple game.

- **Our area is active in resettling refugees.** Families can help with the many tasks involved, such as cleaning an apartment before the family arrives; setting up dishes, towels, dressers; assembling furniture from IKEA; teaching the family the bus system; or being conversation partners.

Extra challenge: Organize a group of friends or neighbors to do this with you!

8

ANIMALS

They don't call them "therapy dogs" for no reason. Our family has a theory that all dogs are therapy dogs because they bring such joy. And the wonders of the animal world extend to the sky and water of the backyard and nearby park as well.

- **Give the dog a bath and haircut.** If you don't own clippers, try to borrow from a friend.

- **Take the dog to the dog park.** Bring water for thirsty dogs and towels for muddy feet.

- **Walk the neighbor's dog,** or your own (bonus: you could earn money).

- **Teach the dogs a trick.** In addition to the useful ones like Sit, Stay, and Come, we like to teach High Five, Tell Me Secrets (snuggle my ear), and Look Happy (turn in circles).

- **Dress up agreeable dogs and cats in funny outfits.**

- **Write silly signs for the dog or cat to sit by.** Examples include "I bark at the delivery man, even though he brings my kibble" or "They want me to chase mice, but I prefer to nap." Take a picture and enjoy the humor.

- **Order butterfly or praying mantis larvae online.** Hatch and release them.

- **Capture tadpoles and watch them turn into frogs.** Make sure to have a humane way of releasing them well before the cold of fall sets in.

- **Look closely at the insects in the backyard.** Look up their names in an insect book. See how many you can identify.

- **Sketch or photograph birds you see in the yard.** Look up their names in bird books. Compile your drawings or photos to make your own bird book.

- **Offer to petsit** for a friend's cat or guinea pig when they go on vacation.

- **Make a bird feeder.** This could be the simple pinecone-with-peanut-butter-and-birdseed, or more complex using scrap wood, nails, and hammer.

- **Choose an animal and photograph it in various settings** (your own pet, or a wild goose, for example).

- **Go horseback riding** or simply sit on a pony while it is lead around a corral.

- **Our library hosts a Country in the City event, and patrons get a chance to touch and see farm animals up close.**

Extra challenge: Foster a dog or cat.

9

CREATE SOMETHING

We'll admit it. As much as we love our traditional school, it doesn't often do much to foster creativity in our children. Schools don't tend to afford the wide swathes of time that are necessary to conceive of, execute, and refine a creative plan. So summer is the perfect time to let our minds wander into something wonderful. It's okay if your first several attempts are not what you are hoping for. Practice makes progress. Here are some ideas to get you on the path to creating something special.

- **Make mudpies and bake them in the sun.**

- **Order** *Bare Books* (blank hardcover books meant for whatever your imagination dreams up) **and keep a journal.**

- **Use a Bare Book to make a board book for a young friend or relative.** Glue in fabric, sandpaper, or feathers for a tactile experience.

- **Grab a camera and embark on a photography project.** Use nature, babies, pets, flowers, or events for inspiration.

- **Sew something.** (see *Tinker* Chapter)

- **Write a story, poem, or song.**

- **Practice your drawing skills** by checking out Ed Emberley books from the library and following the simple exercises there.

- **Use a hot glue gun** to squirt the glue into interesting shapes and make earrings, shoes for Barbie, or other one-of-a-kind accessories.

- **Melt old crayons in molds** for uniquely shaped art supplies.

- **Try different recipes for playdough, slime, or unicorn snot.** See library books for project specifics.

- **Do something amazing with toilet paper rolls.** One idea we like is to fold in about an inch on both sides of one end so it is partially closed off and looks like an owl head. Use a black marker to draw large eyes, a small pointed beak, and lots of curvy feathers for a wise finger puppet.

- **Buy some canvases from a craft store, and use acrylic paint to make an idea come to life.**

- Got yarn, but not up for knitting or crochet? **Learning to finger or arm knit** takes about 3 minutes and can entertain young minds for hours.

- **Melt beeswax and make candles,** using half of a toilet paper roll as a mold. Cotton string makes a simple wick.

- **Glue felt, yarn, feathers, and buttons to socks** to make silly hand puppets.

- **Clip inspirational magazine photos and phrases, and paste to a posterboard** to create a Peace Collage (a collection of best wishes for our world).

- **Unroll a length of butcher paper** and trace a family member, draw a cityscape, write the world's longest poem, or anything else that the giant paper inspires. A paper airplane big enough to carry the cat, for example.

- **Get your hands on a large cardboard box and make a playhouse, spaceship, or tunnel.** If you didn't happen to purchase a large appliance recently, ask around the neighborhood or at a home improvement store. They don't call them "big box" stores for nothin'!

Extra challenge: Check out some Rube Goldberg books from the library and make your own multi-step contraption that completes a very simple task. Feeding the dog, getting the mail, and waking someone up sound like fun.

10

BOARD GAMES

Who needs video games when you have a closet filled with board games, cards, and dice? Sometimes you don't even need those. Let your imagination fly!

- **Play board games outdoors.** Find a shady area or build one yourself with PVC pipe and bedsheets as described in the _Embrace the Outdoors_ chapter.

- **Invite neighbors over to play.** Rainy day equals gamey day!

- **Swap games with friends to play something new-to-you**. No need to get bored of board games when you can trade with another family every week or two.

- **Play oversized versions of favorites** (Jumbo Jenga, for example).

- **Charades get you up and moving.** Play a storebought version, use word cards from other games, or make your own. Themes could be "Books we've all read," "Christmas songs," or, our favorite, "Dogs we've babysat."

- **Make a scavenger hunt.** This could be as simple as drawing pictures for small children to find in the yard or house (draw a spoon, a leaf, a ladybug, and ask kids to find them) or as complex as composing riddles that hint at the items to find ("a puffy white lion" could mean a dandelion, and "a heavy volume" could mean a large book).

- Like to sing? **Play Name That Tune and have different themes:** Christmas carols, songs about nature, songs from your favorite artist, etc. Hum the first few notes and see who guesses first.

- Like the garden? **Play Name That Herb.** Have a partner close his/her eyes. Pick an herb and hold it up for him/her to smell and guess.

Extra challenge: Make your own game based on your interests. You could even make a board game with the list from this book. Whatever space you land on is the activity to do next!

11

GET MOVING

Summer is a great opportunity to get some extra exercise or try a new sport. Physical exercise has also been known to decrease the need for many medications while increasing ability to concentrate and get along with others. We enjoy those endorphins at our house!

- **Take a bus somewhere.** Even a short ride to the library or the grocery store will get you out and about.

- **Walk or run a 5K, or perhaps just a 1 mile fun run.** The excitement of the crowd is infectious and may have you skipping.

- **Ride a bike to your destination** (library, park, store, etc). You could bring a picnic, if you like.

- **Go on a nature walk.** Many city parks have nature trails behind them. Bring a camera or sketchbook to document birds, fish, and turtles you might see.

- **Climb a ropes course.** Not for the faint of heart.

- **Attend a zumba class,** or just dance to Latin music at home.

- **Bounce at an indoor inflatable playscape or trampoline park.**

- **Go to McDonald's playland.** Bonus: it's air-conditioned!

- **Jump rope, hoola hoop, or square dance.** See chapter on *Vintage Fun.*

- **Enjoy a taste of winter by ice skating** at an indoor rink.

- **Create an obstacle course in the backyard, or at the park.**

- **Visit as many municipal pools as you can.**

- **Chores** such as pulling weeds or sweeping the deck are good exercise too, especially when peppy music has you working quickly.

Extra challenge: Organize a kids triathlon and use the proceeds to benefit a local cause.

12

PERFORM MUCH?

Not everyone loves performing, but for those of us who consider the world our stage, summer is a great time to shine. Put some focused time and effort into creating and rehearsing your act, then present it to a backyard audience. Homemade frozen custard or good old fashioned s'mores would be a tasty way to celebrate after the final curtain.

- **Put on a theatrical play.** You might be able to borrow scripts from a school or library. Or write an original work!

- **Join a choir or chorus,** or form one yourself.

- **Learn some simple magic tricks** and dazzle the audience with your new skills.

- **Show off a jump rope, hoola hoop, dance, or gymnastics routine.**

- **Put on a cooking show** and teach the audience to make a tasty summer treat.

- **Play a song** on a musical instrument.

- **Hold a neighborhood dog show** and display Fido's new tricks.

- **Memorize a passage from a famous speech, poem, or other meaningful text.** Perform a dramatic reading.

Extra challenge: Organize a Variety Show with friends or neighbors.

We are about halfway through this manual that empowers you to reduce the time spent on electronic devices in your household. If you have found anything of value here, or if this compilation has caused you to think about summertime in a new light, we encourage you to leave a review on Amazon. Thank you!

13

BUILD COMMUNITY

They say it takes a village to raise a child, so it's important to make an effort to sow into that village and get to know those neighbors. Not only do neighbors look out for each other during the big events (think: flash flooding, crime, downed trees), but they can also lend a hand for the smaller happenings as well (at least once a year, our dog hops the fence and is returned by a friendly neighbor). Summer gives us the opportunity to develop relationships with those who live near us and to bring some cheer to the neighborhood.

- **Use sidewalk chalk to write greetings to neighbors on their sidewalk or driveway.** You could go with the traditional "Good morning!" and "Congrats on the new baby!", or something more unique like "Nice rosebush!" and "You are invited to a picnic at our house tonight!"

- **Hold a neighborhood garage sale.** A time for collective purging!

- Have an elderly neighbor? **Offer to run an errand for him/her.** Or make some iced tea to sip over a nice chat.

- **Take group bike rides.** Try out a new local restaurant. Our town holds a bike tour of all the taquerias, called Tacos On Wheels. The participants look so happy.

- **Volunteer as a group.** Clean up the local park, visit the senior home, or serve the meal at the soup kitchen.

- **Invite friends over for a picnic.** We make it a potluck because often food can be a conversation piece.

- **Show a movie on the side of someone's white garage at dusk**. Does it really count as screentime if you are creating a makeshift drive-in theater? We say, "Nah."

- **Organize a neighborhood picnic or a block party** and invite the whole gang.

- **Participate in a community garden.** Don't have one? You could start your own!

- **Grow food in your front yard.** Display a sign that invites others to take ripe vegetables. This will be sure to start conversations!

- **Install a Little Free Library in your front yard** (see chapter on <u>Unschooling</u> for details). You could even put a little bench nearby to encourage people to linger.

Extra challenge: Paint an old headboard with chalkboard paint, and write jokes/riddles to entertain neighbors.

14

EMBRACE THE OUTDOORS

Warmer temperatures mean more opportunity for time outside. Time to stock up on that vitamin D, but be sure to take breaks in the shade. We find that we sleep more soundly at night when we've had a full day of outdoor activity.

- **Have breakfast outside.** Why? Because you can. And there's nothing like the morning sun to start the day off right.

- **Go berry picking.** In our area, strawberries are available in June, blueberries in July, and raspberries in August. No penalty for eating berries while you pick!

- **Nap outside.** Hang a hammock in the shade and swing yourself to sleep.

- **Play in a tepee.** Tie four or five 5-foot lengths of PVC pipe together near one end and stand it up to make a cone shape. Drape with a bedsheet and secure with clothespins for an easy tepee. Put a picnic blanket on the ground to make a cozy hideaway. Bring books, pillows, and snacks for a fun way to spend a summer day.

- **Have extra PVC?** Use 12 pipes of equal length (we used 5' lengths of pipe that was ¾" thick) and 8 3-way elbow connectors to make a 5-foot cube. Drape it with a bedsheet or two and secure with clothespins for a portable little shade room.

- **Pitch a tent.** Who needs a campground when you have a backyard? Used tents can be found at some secondhand shops or on craigslist. Or maybe at that neighborhood garage sale from the *Build Community* chapter.

- **Clip the bushes.** Even elementary aged kids can be taught to use manual hedge clippers. They can trim the bushes in tidy squares and circles, or clip away a space just big enough for a child to play.

We follow a general guideline at our house: the front yard is tidy and neat, and the backyard can be creative and whimsical. Seems to work.

- **Tend the garden.** There is always a weed to pull, a bloom to dead-head, or some sticks to gather. Even just 10 minutes of focused effort can pay off beautifully.

- **Grow a succulent garden.** Don't have the space for a large garden plot? Want to bring the green inside? Succulents can be grown indoors in containers. Check out library books for inspiration and instruction.

- **Make a rope/tire swing.** Find a sturdy branch, some strong rope, and a tire or piece of wood for a seat. Soon you'll have a spot to spin and swing (which is guaranteed to attract all the neighborhood kids).

- **Build a treehouse.** This one is quite a commitment, but can be done simply. A sturdy tree is key. Get ideas from library books on treehouses. It took about a week to construct ours and we tried to make it a family affair by having the kids participate as much as possible. Our favorite features are the rope ladder and the basket on a pulley. After it's done, bring lunch up there or pillows and books for a lazy afternoon.

Extra challenge: Organize a chalk walk. This is a creative activity that requires a bit of planning. Ahead of time, mark a path through your neighborhood with arrows on the sidewalk drawn in chalk. At points of interest (a cute fairy house, a park bench, a unique tree), draw a star. At street intersections, write a discussion question. Later on, invite a group of kids (or adults too!) to follow the arrows and experience the chalk walk. The idea is for the points of interest and discussion questions to be a catalyst for meaningful conversation. The destination could be a playground, a bonfire, or an ice cream shop. We try to do this as a culminating event before school starts in the fall.

15

UNSCHOOL

While unschooling is a legitimate way for families to approach homeschooling, we use the term to mean any kind of learning that happens outside of the traditional classroom. We take advantage of the summer break from regular school to structure learning in ways that require more flexibility than kids normally get from September to June. I guess we should say that we UNstructure the learning!

- **Do a research project.** Follow your wondering, wandering mind and actually find the answers to all those questions that pop up. Our list includes The Bubonic Plague, Bonsai Trees, Passenger Pigeons, and more. Let the kids roam the library, perusing the nonfiction shelves and asking the librarians questions.

- **Play math games.** Getting bored in the car or standing in line? Start skip counting. One person starts and you go around the circle, each person saying the next multiple of a given number. For example, say "Let's skip count with 4's. I'll start. Four!" "Eight!" "Twelve!" And so on.

- **Everyone loves to laugh.** This game is called "Ha!" You go around the circle, each person saying one more "ha" than the previous person. So basically, you are counting off "ha"s. The first person to laugh is out. For example, the beginner says "ha", the next person says "ha, ha," the next person says "ha, ha, ha," and so on. How high can you go? This activity subtly encourages kids to split up large numbers into smaller groups, sometimes with remainders. Play it and see the thought process unfold.

- **Read for fun.** Give the kids their own library card, a canvas bag, and the freedom to fill it. Summer is a great time to read strictly for pleasure. For a while we had a guideline, the kids could read pretty much any book they wanted (not too grown up, of course) on their own, but we insisted on quality literature for our read-alouds and audiobooks. So together we enjoyed Newbery titles, historical fiction, culturally relevant stories, and local authors. Sometimes we hit the jackpot and found a book that met all these goals: pretty much anything by Christopher Paul Curtis (he's from Flint, MI)!

• **Read for benefit.** Instead of (or in addition to) paying kids to clean toilets or wash windows (tasks that will train them for minimum wage jobs as adults), consider paying them to read nonfiction books about personal development, entrepreneurship, or a skill they are interested in developing. We require them to also give a short presentation about what they learned and feel this type of "chore" will have lasting benefit for them.

• **Spelling challenges.** Sit the kids down cross-legged on the floor. The adult has a bowl of pretzels, grapes, pennies, or other small treats and at least one book that each child has read (or a proper spelling list, if you prefer more structure). One by one, the adult selects a word from the child's book or list and asks him/her to spell it, spelling bee style. Other options are to have the kids write the word on a whiteboard or arrange it with Scrabble tiles. A correct answer earns the child one of the treats. The child needs to "pay back" one of the treats to the leader for an incorrectly spelled word. After about 10 or so words for each child, end the game and enjoy the treats together. My kids (and even a neighbor child) still find this fun and they are in middle school.

• **Map work.** There was a fateful day last year when one of the kids asked if New Orleans was a state. We knew right then that they were not getting a proper geography education and made a point to unschool this subject over the summer. Specifically, I took them to the library, handed them a blank map of the US, and instructed them to find an atlas in order to fill in the map with all 50 states and capitals. We then set about memorizing them. Each day I handed them another blank map and asked them to fill in 5 states and capitals from memory. The next day it was another blank map and 5 more (10 states and capitals total). The following day, 5 more, and so on. There was only minimal complaining and a whole lot of empowerment. And now they can point to Louisiana on any map. The other day, one of them asked where Spain was, so you can guess what kind of map they'll be working with this summer!

- **Bible verses.** The break from traditional school allows for more time to dive into other disciplines. There is more to life that reading, writing, and 'rithmetic, so feel free to embrace the sacred text of your faith and tuck some of it away in your heart. Challenge each other to memorize key passages. Act them out. Draw them. Follow inspiration from the text to engage in a special way.

- **Inspirational quotes and speeches.** The hard work of memorizing sections of text impacts the brain in a unique way. Will you choose Martin Luther King, Jr.? Abraham Lincoln? Shakespeare? If you are feeling brave, you could display your efforts in the Variety Show mentioned in the chapter on *performing*.

- **Money matters.** Do the kids ever see you pay bills? Where do they think the ATM gets all its cash? Do they have a working knowledge of deposits and withdrawals, interest and charitable giving? The chapter on *starting a business* might have left them with some funds to handle, so a trip to the bank may be in order. Even young children understand that money can be saved or used for good purposes. It's never too early to learn that money doesn't grow on trees, but instead can be earned and used wisely. So get those conversations started! This could be one of the most useful lessons they will take with them to adulthood.

- **Little Free Libraries.** Has your community discovered Little Free Libraries? They are exactly that: large mailbox-type structures outside of people's homes, at the park, or near a business. And they are filled with books! The idea is that anyone can simply take a book, or leave a book. No library card, no fines, no checkout slip. There are about 15 in our town and one summer we got our hands on a list of them and visited them all. We did this in conjunction with purging our own book stash, so we felt good about leaving a stack of books for others to discover.

Extra challenge: Host a skill share in which you decide on a skill you'd like to teach, and invite interested friends to come and learn. Kids can do this too. Are they good at making chocolate chip cookies? They can host a small baking class. Do other kids marvel at their jump roping skills? Host a little lesson. Plan ahead and ask participants to bring the supplies they'll need.

16

NEW FOODS

Food can be so fun! Let summer be the chance to try something new. Cuisine can be a tangible and tasty way to engage another culture as well. Are your kids not so eager? Most cultures have some type of rice and bread, and we've yet to meet a kid who doesn't love those. It's ok to ease into it.

Staying home to eat? Give those kids a job! Even the little ones can wash veggies or sprinkle on spices. Older kids can take more ownership and plan the bulk of the meal, even use knives, stoves, and ovens with supervision. They say that kids who help prepare the meal will eat more of it.

- **Go ethnic.** We've got Middle Eastern, Central American, Asian restaurants of all kinds near us. What's near you?

- **Go ethnic at home.** Libraries have a variety of cookbooks that provide a great way to experience another culture. Did you enjoy something you ate at a restaurant? You could try making it at home. We've also heard of increasing global awareness through food. You could choose one country where US troops are stationed, research the local cuisine, and make some of the signature dishes.

- **Grill something new** (asparagus, pizza, lettuce, potatoes). Libraries usually have grilling cookbooks too. Or you could keep it simple and roast a hotdog on a skewer over an open fire.

- **Homemade ice cream.** You don't need fancy machines for this. Research frozen custard for a simple, refreshing dessert. Our favorite recipe calls for just eggs, honey, and cream.

- **Something from the garden.** Lettuce and spinach are incredibly easy to grow in early summer. Carrots are a fun surprise to pull from the dirt. And tomatoes from the garden are so heavenly you'll want to write poetry. We make a list of foods that we enjoy that could be expensive at the store, and grew those. We buy seedlings from a local garden shop and don't bother with growing from seeds. In our area, even June 1 is not too late to get a seedling into the soil.

- **Drive-in restaurant.** These old fashioned gems won't serve the healthiest of foods, but the fare is tasty and fun. Hanging a tray of food on the car window will be a unique memory for sure. Three final words on this: Root Beer Floats!

- **Try a food truck.** It's adventurous to look at the menu painted on the side of a vehicle, order from a face sticking out of the side of a vehicle, then eat standing up beside that vehicle. Our town has one called Jamerican Grill, serving what I assume is a Jamaican-American fusion, and a more ambiguous one called Stuff Your Belly. What food trucks have you seen around town?

- **Get adventurous at the grocery store.** Have certain foods always caught your eye, but you've never gotten around to trying them? Why not try them now? Foods that we've bought on a whim: star fruit, ugli fruit, fennel, ground buffalo, plantains, and Mexican sweets made of annatto seeds.

Extra challenge: Create a new cupcake flavor combination. We've seen flavors like Blueberry Lemon and Maple Bacon. Use a basic white or chocolate cake recipe and add your own ideas. What flavor combo sounds fun to you?

17

HOME IMPROVEMENT

Entropy: a scientifically proven fact that there is a gradual decline into disorder. Without general maintenance, our homes deteriorate a tiny bit at a time. So we act against that decline and we teach our children to fix items that are broken, clean things that are dirty, and improve areas that are in need.9

- **Purge closets and dressers.** It feels great when the drawer closes smoothly, and you can find the articles you are looking for. The key is getting rid of items that you do not love. So be ruthless and keep only the items that you truly use and enjoy.

- **Sell or donate contents.** Holding a garage sale or donating to a charity is a great way to dispose of these items. Many charities will pick up bags of clothes and household goods right from your doorstep.

- **Spring cleaning, not just for spring.** Between birthdays, holidays, and concerts, we often get otherwise occupied in the spring. So the foyer doesn't get scrubbed till June sometimes. And the deck doesn't get washed till school is out. No problem. Choose a room, enlist the kids, and tackle it together.

- **Improve the mailbox.** Give it a fresh coat of paint, or plant some flowers nearby. Perhaps it needs more creative decorating, like glow-in-the-dark house numbers or festive stickers.

- **Hang a hammock.** Nothing says "summer" like a hammock hung between two trees. Grab a glass of lemonade and a good book to break it in.

- **Create a garden area or spruce up an old one.** Whether it be a flower bed or a strawberry patch, gardens need tending. Each child could have their own garden area to plan and tend. Or the family could tackle a larger project together, such as a vertical garden.

- **Install solar lighting outdoors.** Kids can line a sidewalk with lights or place them around a garden area. Help them hang a string of lights over the deck or near the front door.

- **Take family photos, frame them, hang them.** Bonus: you'll be ready when it's time to send holiday cards.

- **Paint a room.** Nothing says, "I love it here!" like a fresh coat of paint.

- **Looming project.** Is there something that's been on your list for a while now? Building a loft in the kids' bedroom? Finishing part of the basement into a rec room? Pulling out overgrown shrubs? Knock it out together!

> **Extra challenge:** Turn an unused shed into a playhouse. Or repurpose some scrap lumber into a tepee. Line the floor with landscaping stones.

18

RELATIONSHIPS

We all know that quality relationships take time to develop and an effort to sustain. Let the freedom of the summer schedule allow you to sow into relationships that are important to you. People do get busy, so it's best to start planning early to make sure you connect in a meaningful way.

- **Write letters.** Make some fun stationary with stamps and jot a note to a friend near or far. You could include photos, stickers, or an activity page. Some say the handwritten letter is a dying art, but it is so fun to receive a personal note in the mail. Another piece of family lore states that when the grandparents were courting in the 1960s, they played the game Battleship over the mail, with each letter containing the next move. How long that game must have taken!

- **Visit long lost family and friends.** Those buddies you haven't seen since they moved away, those cousins you enjoyed at the last reunion, those classmates that switched schools. Give them a call and find a time to share a meal, a walk, or even a road trip.

- **Establish a penpal.** Yes, you might have to initially set this up on-line, but the actual letters can be exchanged via snail mail. Decide if you want to practice a foreign language this way, or if you'd like your penpal to practice his/her English. What a unique chance to connect with someone from another state or even country!

- **Spend the night at the grandparents' house.** My kids still love a sleepover with Gramma and Grampa. Special breakfasts, different outings, quiet time for parents, and a larger perspective on our family make these events beneficial for all involved.

- **Date Night, with your child.** Carve out time for one-on-one appointments with each child. This does not have to be elaborate or expensive. It can be as simple as a trip to the park. Let the child choose from a few activities. Ask the child getting-to-know-you questions, like you might on a first date. You might be surprised at what his/her favorite color is this week!

Extra challenge: Sponsor a child through a charity and send letters, coloring pages, and photos. You could also research the child's country and make this an unschooling activity as well.

19

THEMED PARTIES

Want to have a playdate, but need something to make it a tad more fun? Invite friends over for a themed lunch, potluck style! Choose a type of food and invite everyone to bring their favorite version. Anything goes!

- **Salad party.** The word "salad" can be as loosely defined as you like.

- **Taco party.** Let people get creative about what they put in those tortillas.

- **Popcorn party.** Simple butter, sweet cinnamon sugar, or sassy sriracha are common toppings at our house.

- **Pizza party.** Pizza is pretty much anything on a flatbread, right?

- **Pasta party.** Al forno, stuffed, or good ol' mac'n'cheese.

- **Fruit and nut party.** A plate of fruit and a bowl of nuts makes a simple lunch at our house.

- **P party.** Invite friends over to eat foods that start with the letter P, play games that start with P, listen to music by people whose names start with P.

- **Toothpick party.** Serve food that can be eaten with toothpicks. Think: fruit salad, sandwich kabobs, mini sausages, cheese cubes. We believe every food is fancy when it's eaten on a toothpick.

- **Breakfast for dinner. Or lunch.** Who doesn't love omelettes, bacon, and chocolate chip pancakes any time of day?

- **Locavore lunch.** Serve food that was grown, raised, and harvested within 100 miles. Take the pressure off by making this a potluck. Your local farmers' market and food co-op can help you find what you need (or more likely, offer alternatives).

Extra challenge: The dramatic overachievers among us might enjoy hosting a mystery dinner party. Older kids and adults can participate in taking on an assigned identity with the goal of piecing together clues to solve a crime by the end of the evening. These plots can be purchased as a kit. Make it a potluck so your energy can be focused on the sleuthing.

20

TINKER A BIT

Studies have shown that adults who played with Legos as kids make better engineers, and those who can use a needle and thread make better surgeons and nurses. So get those little hands moving and make something. Even preschoolers can stack blocks and stitch on sewing cards.

- **Craft kits.** Craft stores have made it very easy for parents who don't consider themselves very creative. And the coupons that the stores offer make those kits affordable. We've seen kits for candle-making, weaving on a loom, garden stones, simple sewing, bead-work, fairy gardens, origami, string art, friendship bracelets, foamy mosaics, and so many more!

- **Subscription to tinker kits by mail.** There are companies that will send you a monthly kit with instructions and all the materials you need to build various projects. We've seen kits that will have your kids working with two-way mirrors, pulleys, fiber optics, gears, magnets, with no creativity needed on the part of the parent at all.

- **Sew something.** Thread that needle and get to stitching something simple. Ideas include a pillowcase, stuffed animal, purse, tool belt, puppet, cape. Libraries often have books on simple sewing projects. Older kids can learn to use the sewing machine and tackle more involved projects.

- **Make something with duct tape.** Join the duct tape craze by making a wallet, a headband, or slippers from regular gray duct tape. Or splurge for some neon colored or leopard print tape. We've seen books at the library with step-by-step instructions.

- **Marble run on a wall.** Use painter's tape to fasten toilet paper tubes to the wall in a zigzag fashion. Drop a marble in the top to create a wall-mounted marble run.

- **Do you have a large fallen branch after the winter and spring** storms? Cut it up into discs to make circular blocks. Kids can sand the ends, then stack them to make towers, cities, or whatever else they imagine. Alternatively, they could use a woodburning tool to write or draw something on the cut ends (with parent supervision).

- **Build a fairy door.** Make one from scratch or buy one from a hobby store and embellish it with plastic jewels, paint, or pebbles. Mount it at the base of a tree. See who leaves little trinkets for the fairies to find.

- **Make a periscope.** Explain the concept of a periscope and hand them 2 small mirrors, some sturdy cardboard, and of course some tape. Stand back and see what they come up with .

- **Take a hint from the business world and ask the kids to build a tower out of dried spaghetti and marshmallows.** This activity is aimed to draw out leadership skills and creativity.

- **Are the kids already noisy?** See if they can make their own musical instruments. An oatmeal container can be a drum, fishing line and a box can be a guitar, and tissue paper over a comb can be a harmonica. Viola! Homemade band!

Extra challenge: Turn 'em loose with supplies. Some friends of ours turned an unused space in their house into a Make Lab. They stocked it with various supplies so the kids could build whatever came to mind. They had on hand paper, tape, markers, staplers, toilet paper tubes, buttons, pipe cleaners, and egg cartons. As the kids got older they moved the Make Lab to their garage and added hammers, nails, drills, sandpaper, and handsaws. Those kids came to school with some very unique projects!

21

WATER FUN

The heat of the summer is the perfect excuse for cooling off in a swimsuit. Bring some ice water and sunscreen.

- **Sprinkler**. Water yourself and the lawn by running through the sprinkler.

- **Water balloons.** See how many tosses the balloon will last before splashing on someone. We played this last summer at the exact moment when our mailman was making his delivery and he made sure to take a WIDE route around us.

- **Make a water balloon launcher.** Rig up a slingshot of sorts by fastening a funnel to strips of elastic. A hot glue gun is our preferred tool for odd adhesive jobs like this one. Then tie the ends of the elastic to a sturdy Y-shaped branch or thin pieces of scrap wood made into a handle. Set the water balloon in the funnel, pull back, and release!

- **Don't have room for a pool in your backyard?** A kiddie pool can be fun even if the kids have seemingly outgrown it. You can put it up on a picnic table, and kids can float homemade boats in it. They can do science experiments and see how long it take for ice cubes to melt when it is different temperatures outside (morning, high noon, late afternoon).

- **Neighborhood pool.** Does your city have a municipal pool? Or maybe there is a friend who will invite you to their neighborhood pool? You could make it your mission to visit as many as possible throughout the season.

- **Wash the dog**. This might not be Fido's idea of a fun afternoon, but he will smell like roses afterward. He would probably enjoy a walk around the block as a reward, and his fur might also be dry by then.

- **Floaty fun.** Put water in a some bowls and gather some household or garden items. See what floats and what doesn't. What floats at first, but sinks later? Ideas include buttons, corks, pebbles, flower petals, herbs, Barbie shoes, sponges, wood chips, dog food, you name it. To extend this into a classification exercise, have the children divide up the items into 3 groups: what floats, what sinks, what floats at first but sinks later.

- **Glacier play.** Freeze small toys, trinkets, and coins in blocks of ice the day before. Kids can play with the ice blocks in a kiddie pool or bucket as the ice melts and the items are freed from the ice. They can poke and prod and pretend they are excavating.

- **Did you build the wallside marble run from the chapter on _tin-kering_?** Kids can do something similar outside with water. Cut the bottoms out of plastic containers and drill holes in tin cans. Help kids fasten them to a vertical board in a zig zag design. Then they can pour water in from the top and watch it travel down the water run.

- **Colors of the rainbow.** Use food coloring or a few drops of paint to mix up 3 bowls of water: red, yellow, and blue. Give the kids extra cups, ladles, and bowls and have them combine these primary colors to get green, purple, and orange. What other colors can they make?

- **Wash something.** Our kids love the hose, some soap, and a couple of scrub brushes. This could be practical (like cleaning the cooler before a road trip) or just for fun (like giving all the dolls and toy trucks a bath).

> **Extra challenge:** Create an obstacle course that runs under the sprinkler, through the kiddie pool, and involves catching a water balloon.

22

STAYCATION

Need something fun to do, but aren't quite up for a road trip? How about taking a vacation in your own town? We already mentioned several ideas for *day trips.* Here are more suggestions for making the most of your hometown.

- **Library events.** Ours has a wide selection of musicians, magicians, workshops, and presentations for all ages.

- **Park**. Walk or bike to your favorite one, or try a new one altogether.

- **Backyard camping.** Pitch that tent and pretend you are at the Grand Canyon. Cook all your meals over a campfire.

- **Cushion fort.** Use the couch cushions and bed pillows as building blocks on a rainy staycation day. Eat lunch in there.

- **Eat outdoors.** My kids seem to think that eating a meal in an unconventional place is super special.

- **Local music festivals.** Bring the picnic basket and eat dinner there (see previous point).

- Like soccer, football, or kickball? **Spray lines on the lawn and mark out a proper field.**

- **Check out what's going on at the local university.** Ours has an impressive marching band that practices outdoors in August. It's fun to bring a picnic and watch them work up their shows.

- **Take a tour of the fairy doors.** Has this trend swept your town like it has ours? There are maps that show all the fairy doors around the city. Walk or bike to a few of them, and remember to bring shiny coins, plastic jewels, or flower petals to leave for the tiny residents.

- **Host a visitor and show off the best parts of your town.** This might also help you revisit some of your old favorites.

- **Create a scavenger hunt** that takes a group of friends all over your town, looking for random information gleaned from statues, libraries, signs, restaurant menus, bus maps, street names, convenience stores, etc. An example of a clue might be "Head towards the sunset and turn right on the first street with a compound word." Or while at a certain drug store, "Find the price something you use to cushion your neck during plane rides and multiply it by 60."

Extra challenge: Go to farmers' market and cook a day's meals from ingredients purchased there.

23

DOWNTIME

Need a break? Need some space to think your own thoughts? We admit that we have resorted to devices to provide some relief from being "on" all the time. Both kids and adults benefit from downtime and the opportunity to relax. Here are some relaxing ideas that don't require a screen.

- **Give the kids a pomegranate and pop in a book on CD.**

- **Listen to an old fashioned radio show.** The library may have collections of radio shows on CD.

- **Read a classic story aloud to each other.**

- **Our kids are well past the age of needing a nap, but we still all enjoy an after-lunch rest time.** We read, draw, or collect our thoughts for the rest of the day ahead.

- **Turn on some relaxing music or nature sounds and sit in silence for a short time.** Encourage kids (and adults!) to focus on aspects of their lives they are thankful for.

- **Send them outside to shuck the corn for dinner.** See the chapter on _Life Skills_ for more practical ideas like this.

- **Kid swap.** Trade babysitting with another like-minded family. All the kids come to your house one day, and go to their house later in the week.

- **Overnight at Grandma's.** That's what grandparents are for, right?

Extra challenge: Perhaps you've heard all the benefits of meditation. Try it with the kids. Keep it short at first, maybe just 1 minute. Have them focus on deep breathing. They can use the time for prayer, meditating on an inspirational quote, or simply letting their minds wander. We like to do this in the morning or right after lunch as part of our daily routine. Try to lengthen the time as the summer goes on.

24

FABULOUS FLOPS

As wonderful as all these ideas may sound, we have had our share of failures as well. But even those can be memorable and worthwhile. Commiserate with us as we share some of the not-so-wonderful attempts at screen-free activities.

- The kids insisted on holding a garage sale. They dragged a table to the front yard and set out all of their unwanted items. They sold ZERO of them.

- They attempted to start a business by baking artisan bread and giving samples of it to neighbors with the intent of taking orders and funding their college educations this way. They sold THREE loaves of bread, and we FORGOT to bake one of them on time.

- Dad doesn't like it when our chickens make their messes on the deck, so we got up early on Father's Day to construct a rope fence as a surprise for him. Our plans and materials were not the greatest and, SURPRISE, the chickens still made their messes on the deck.

- We made a really cool tepee from scrap lumber, but it BLEW DOWN in a wind storm.

- We bought a special pan to make cupcakes in the shape of bowls, but they all STUCK TO THE PAN and we had to tear them all up to get them out.

- We tried to learn a foreign language one summer and were very excited for the first 2 or 3 lessons. But then we lost interest and never really continued. How do you say, "I QUIT" in Italian?

- We made some very ambitious egg-shaped truffles one Easter and set the chocolate-dipped results on a mesh cooling rack. The chocolate hardened and essentially GLUED the treats to the rack.

- We saved halves of egg shells to make tiny little planters. We drew little faces on the outside of the shells and put soil and seeds on the inside. The seeds were supposed to grow and look like hair. Then we NEVER WATERED THEM. EVER.

- One of us was working with a stapler and STAPLED HER FINGER.

- One of us was trying to make a Blueberry Buckle recipe healthier by sneaking some pureed spinach in there, only to remember later that that spinach had some GARLIC in it.

- We invited another girl to join us on a museum outing and our two daughters FOUGHT OVER HER the whole time.

- We invited another family over for a game night, not realizing that their children suffer from social anxiety, especially around anything REMOTELY COMPETITIVE.

- One summer we asked the librarian to compile a list of all the children's books that had recipes associated with them. We planned to read the book then make the recipe. Our plans came to a halt when she handed us a list containing OVER 100 BOOKS! *Cranberry Summer* and *Thundercake* were enough for us.

- One spring we invited some friends over to color Easter eggs with natural dyes. We used beets, onion skins, and blueberries. All 3 dozen eggs ended up being various shades of OLIVE GREEN.

- We tried to be all healthy by making pudding with avocados and cocoa. Except it ended up tasting like AVOCADOS MIXED WITH COCOA, not awesome.

CONCLUSION AND INVITATION

So there you have it: 261 ideas for getting kids (and parents) off the device and into the season. And an invitation to expand upon these ideas, follow your curiosities, and discover the world around you.

If you have found any value here, we invite you to leave a review on Amazon. Also feel free to encourage and be encouraged by sharing your experiences of your own screen-free (or less-screen) summer on our facebook page *Screen-Free Summer: Endless Ideas book*. Or, better yet, avoid the irony altogether by sharing the impact that *Screen-Free Summer* has had on your family with a friend or neighbor over an iced tea at the local park.

43902526R00039

Made in the USA
Middletown, DE
22 May 2017